LARGE SEA CREATURES

THE SEA

Jason Cooper

The Rourke Corporation, Inc.
Vero Beach, Florida 32964

Edited by Sandra A. Robinson

PHOTO CREDITS
All photos © Lynn M. Stone

LIBRARY OF CONGRESS
Library of Congress Cataloging-in-Publication Data
Cooper, Jason, 1942-
   Large sea creatures / by Jason Cooper.
   p. cm. — (Discovery library of the sea)
   Includes index.
   Summary: Describes some of the species of large fish, mammals,
reptiles, and birds that live in and around the world's oceans.
   ISBN 0-86593-231-X
   1. Marine fauna—Juvenile literature. [1. Marine animals.] I. Title.
II. Series: Cooper, Jason, 1942-   Discovery library of the sea.
QL122.2.C658   1992
591.92—dc20   92-16072
                         CIP
                         AC

Printed in the USA

TABLE OF CONTENTS

LARGE SEA CREATURES

The sea doesn't actually produce mermaids or monsters. It does, however, produce some large, and often quite strange, creatures.

Several different groups of large animals have found ways to live on or in the sea. The sea is home for **species,** or kinds, of large fish, mammals, reptiles and birds.

While all of these animals are different, life in the sea has made almost all of them alike in one way: They power themselves through the water with either fins, flippers or webbed feet.

Harbor seal's flippers and torpedo-shaped body make it a true sea animal

SALTWATER FISH

Scientists place ocean, or **marine,** fish into two major groups. One group includes fish with skeletons of real bone.

Some of the largest bony fish are king salmon, grouper, tarpon, halibut, marlin and tuna. The bluefin tuna, which can weigh about 1,500 pounds, is the largest of the bony fish.

A tarpon, the "Silver King" of the sea

SHARKS AND RAYS

Sharks and rays, or skates, belong to the second major group of fish. These fish have no bones. Their skeletons are made of a flexible material called **cartilage.** You have cartilage in the bridge of your nose.

The largest fish in the world is the whale shark. It can be 45 feet long and weigh 30,000 pounds.

Rays usually live on the sea bottom. However, the largest ray, the manta or devil ray, often swims along the ocean surface.

A skate, or ray,
washed up on a Florida beach

PORPOISES AND WHALES

Porpoises (sometimes called dolphins) and whales are marine mammals, just as humans and cats are land mammals.

Like other mammals, porpoises and whales breathe air, produce milk for their babies, and have hair sometime during their lives.

Porpoises and whales are known as **cetaceans.** The cetaceans range in size from a five-foot species of porpoise to the blue whale, which can be 100 feet long and weigh 300,000 pounds.

Bottle-nosed porpoise and other cetaceans live in the sea but surface to breathe

Giant sea turtles come ashore only to lay their eggs

Atlantic puffins live on seaside cliffs and dive to catch small marine fish

SEALS

Seals are marine mammals, too. But unlike cetaceans, seals are not totally animals of the ocean. Seals leave the ocean to rest and have their babies.

Seals have smooth, torpedo-shaped bodies, so they can swim and dive extremely well.

More seals live in the icy Antarctic Ocean than anywhere else in the world. Their fat and fur keep them warm.

The elephant seal and walrus are the largest seals, each weighing up to about 8,000 pounds.

Huge elephant seal bulls roar challenges near a California beach

SEA OTTERS

Despite having webbed feet instead of flippers, like other sea mammals, sea otters rarely leave the ocean. Their thick fur keeps them warm.

Sea otters **prey** upon, or eat, crabs, squid, sea urchins and abalones, which are clamlike animals.

A sea otter is one of the very few animals to use "tools." While floating on its back, the sea otter uses stones to crack open shelled animals that it holds against its chest.

Once nearly killed off for their sleek fur, sea otters have made a slow return

MANATEES

The West Indian manatee of Florida and the Caribbean Sea looks like a giant gray barrel with flippers.They grow fat (up to 1,800 pounds) on a diet of sea plants.

Manatees are gentle, slow-moving mammals that live in shallow, warm sea water. In winter, many of them swim into freshwater rivers.

Manatees are often struck by speedboats and either killed or injured. Partly for that reason, manatees have become **endangered**—in danger of disappearing altogether, or becoming **extinct.**

West Indian manatee is one of the most endangered sea mammals

SEA BIRDS

Sea birds spend all or part of the year hunting at sea. Sea birds may dive deep into the water, like penguins or cormorants, or pluck food from the surface, as gulls and petrels do.

Sea birds have webbed feet and water-proofed feathers to help them swim.

Many sea birds, like pelicans, eat only fish. Others catch a variety of sea creatures. Penguins eat krill, a type of shrimp.

*Brown pelican lives on shore,
but dives for ocean fish*

SEA TURTLES

Sea turtles spend their entire lives at sea, except when females crawl ashore to nest.

Sea turtles can weigh several hundred pounds. They are slow and awkward on land, but their flippers and streamlined shells make them excellent swimmers.

Sea snakes are reptile cousins of the turtles. They are highly poisonous but they rarely bite anyone.

Sea snakes live in the Indian Ocean and in the warmer parts of the Pacific.

Glossary

cartilage (KART ul ij) — strong, flexible substance produced instead of bone by certain organisms

cetacean (seh TAY shun) — a group of largely marine mammals including dolphins, porpoises and whales

endangered (en DANE jerd) — in danger of no longer existing

extinct (ex TINKT) — no longer existing

marine (muh REEN) — of or relating to the sea, salt water

prey (PRAY) — an animal that is hunted by another for food

species (SPEE sheez) — within a group of closely related animals, such as whales, one certain kind or type (*blue* whale)

INDEX